The Wealth Habit
A Practical 6-Week Blueprint to Transform Your Finances and Build Lasting Riches

BY
Stanton Rollins

CONTENTS

INTRODUCTION 1
Welcome to Financial Freedom..2

Part 1:..9
Laying the Foundation for Financial Success 9

Chapter 01..10
Defining Your Wealth Vision 10
Chapter 02..17
Assessing Your Current Financial Reality 17
Chapter 03..25
Mastering the Wealth Mindset..25

PART 2:..33
Taking Control of Your Finances 33

Chapter 04..34
Building an Effective Budget...34
Chapter 05..42
Slashing Debt the Smart Way 42
Chapter 06..49
Establishing a Financial Safety Net...................................49

Part 3:..56
Growing and Protecting Your Wealth.............................56

Chapter 07..57
Mastering the Basics of Investing 57
....57
Chapter 08..64
Increasing Your Income Streams 64

Chapter 09..74
Protecting Your Wealth from Risks 74

Part 4:...**86**
Sustaining Your Wealth Habit............................**86**

Chapter 10..87
Automating Your Finances for Success............87
Chapter 11..99
Tracking Progress and Adjusting Strategies 99
Chapter 12..110
Paying It Forward and Leaving a Legacy.......110

Conclusion **122**
The Wealth Habit for Life..................................**123**

INTRODUCTION

Welcome to Financial Freedom

Congratulations! You've taken the first step toward transforming your financial life. Whether you're struggling to make ends meet, drowning in debt, or simply yearning for a sense of control over your money, you've picked up the right book. "The Wealth Habit" isn't just a guide—it's a blueprint for reshaping how you think about, manage, and grow your finances. By the end of this journey, you'll be equipped with the habits and strategies to achieve lasting financial freedom.

Overview of the Book's Purpose and Promise

Think for a moment about what financial freedom means to you. Does it mean living without the constant stress of bills? Having the freedom to pursue your passions without worrying about money? Or perhaps it's about building wealth to create a legacy for your family. Whatever your vision, this book is designed to help you get there.

- **The purpose of this book** is to provide you with a step-by-step plan to break free from financial stress, build lasting habits, and grow your wealth sustainably.
- **The promise** is that by the end of these six weeks, you'll not only have a clearer understanding of your finances but also a solid foundation of habits that will serve you for the rest of your life.

This isn't a quick fix, a get-rich-quick scheme, or a generic money management book. Instead, it's a

practical and actionable guide to transform your relationship with money, one habit at a time.

The Mindset Shift: Building Habits, Not Quick Fixes

Most people approach finances with the wrong mindset. They look for shortcuts—tips, tricks, and hacks—that promise quick results but fail to create lasting change. Let's be honest: if there were a magic formula for instant wealth, wouldn't everyone be financially free?

Here's the truth: financial success isn't about what you know—it's about what you do **consistently**. Knowledge is important, but without action, it's useless. This book focuses on building sustainable habits because habits, not one-time efforts, are the true building blocks of wealth.

- **Habits are the secret to consistency.** Small, daily actions compound over time, leading to big results.
- **Why quick fixes fail:** They rely on motivation, which is fleeting, rather than discipline and systems.
- **The habit-building advantage:** Once a habit is formed, it requires less effort to maintain, freeing up your mental energy for bigger goals.

For example, consider the habit of saving. Saving $5 a day may seem insignificant, but over a year, that's $1,825. Add compound interest, and the growth becomes exponential. This book teaches you how to incorporate such habits into your daily life effortlessly.

Why Traditional Money Advice Often Fails

There's no shortage of financial advice out there: books, podcasts, YouTube channels, social media influencers. Yet, many people still struggle with money. Why? Because traditional advice often overlooks one critical factor: **real life**.

Common Problems with Traditional Advice

1. **One-size-fits-all solutions:** Most financial advice assumes that everyone's situation is the same. But your financial goals, challenges, and resources are unique.
2. **Overemphasis on knowledge:** Knowing about budgeting or investing isn't enough if you don't know how to apply it consistently.
3. **Lack of focus on habits:** Advice like "just save more" or "cut your spending" doesn't address the underlying behaviors that cause financial struggles.
4. **Unrealistic expectations:** Many programs expect drastic changes overnight, which can feel overwhelming and unsustainable.

This book takes a different approach. It focuses on **building personalized habits** that fit your life and empower you to take control of your finances step by step.

Introducing the 6-Week Plan: A New Approach

Imagine having a clear, manageable plan to improve your finances over just six weeks. That's exactly what this book offers. Each week focuses on a specific aspect of financial growth, from understanding your current situation to creating systems that sustain your progress.

Why Six Weeks?

- **Short enough to feel achievable:** Six weeks is a manageable time frame to stay focused and motivated.
- **Long enough to create real change:** Research shows it takes about 30-60 days to form a new habit.

What You'll Achieve in Six Weeks

- Week 1: Understanding where you are financially.
- Week 2: Setting clear, actionable goals.
- Week 3: Building a realistic budget that works for you.
- Week 4: Developing strategies to reduce debt and increase savings.
- Week 5: Learning the basics of investing and growing your wealth.
- Week 6: Creating systems to sustain your financial habits for life.

Each week is designed to build on the last, ensuring steady progress without feeling overwhelming.

Preview of the Book's Structure and 4-Part System

The book is divided into four parts, each targeting a critical stage in your financial journey:

Part 1: Laying the Foundation for Financial Success

- ➢ Understand your current financial situation and set clear, inspiring goals.
- ➢ Develop the mindset and motivation to stick with the process.

Part 2: Taking Control of Your Finances

- ➢ Learn to budget effectively and tackle debt strategically.
- ➢ Build an emergency fund to protect yourself from unexpected expenses.

Part 3: Growing and Protecting Your Wealth

- ➢ Discover the basics of investing and explore ways to grow your income.
- ➢ Protect your wealth through smart risk management and planning.

Part 4: Sustaining Your Wealth Habit

- ➢ Automate your finances for long-term success.
- ➢ Track your progress and adjust your strategies as needed.

Each chapter provides actionable steps, relatable examples, and practical tools to ensure your success.

How to Commit to Lasting Change

Transformation doesn't happen by accident—it requires commitment. But commitment doesn't mean perfection. It means showing up for yourself, even when it's hard, and trusting the process.

Tips for Staying Committed

1. **Focus on progress, not perfection:** Small, consistent steps will get you further than occasional big leaps.
2. **Celebrate your wins:** Acknowledge every milestone, no matter how small.
3. **Find an accountability partner:** Share your journey with someone who supports and encourages you.
4. **Be kind to yourself:** Financial transformation is a marathon, not a sprint.
5. **Keep your "why" in mind:** Remind yourself of the life you're working to create.

By the end of this book, you'll have not only transformed your finances but also gained the confidence and clarity to build a life of abundance.

Final Thoughts

Welcome to the start of your journey to financial freedom. The fact that you're reading this means you're ready for change—and that's a powerful first step. This book is here to guide, support, and inspire you. Together, we'll build the habits and strategies that will lead to a life of wealth, security, and freedom. Let's begin!

Part 1: Laying the Foundation for Financial Success

Chapter 01

Defining Your Wealth Vision

If you don't know where you're going, how will you know when you get there? That's the core principle behind creating a clear and compelling vision for your financial future. Without a well-defined destination, it's easy to get lost in day-to-day financial decisions or give up when challenges arise. This chapter will guide you through the process of shaping your wealth vision—a roadmap to the life you truly want.

Understanding the Importance of Clear Financial Goals

Financial goals are more than just numbers on a page—they're the foundation of your financial journey. Clear goals provide:

- **Direction:** A roadmap for your efforts. When you know what you're working toward, it's easier to make decisions and stay motivated.
- **Focus:** Goals help you prioritize. Instead of feeling overwhelmed by endless financial tasks, you can concentrate on what matters most.
- **Accountability:** Goals keep you honest about your progress. They show whether you're on track or need to make adjustments.

Imagine setting out on a road trip without a destination in mind. You might enjoy the scenery, but you'll likely waste time and fuel. The same applies to your finances. Clear financial goals give your efforts purpose and prevent aimless spending or saving.

Visualizing Your Ideal Financial Future

Visualization is a powerful tool for creating clarity and motivation. It involves imagining your desired outcome in vivid detail, making it feel more tangible and achievable.

Exercise: Picture Your Financial Dream Life

Take a moment to close your eyes and imagine your ideal financial future. Ask yourself:

- Where are you living?
- How do you spend your days?
- What kind of experiences can you afford for yourself and your family?
- Are you debt-free? Do you have a robust savings account or investments?

Write these answers down. By creating a clear mental image, you'll have a destination to work toward.

Creating SMART Financial Goals

While dreaming big is essential, achieving those dreams requires actionable steps. This is where SMART goals come in. SMART stands for:

- **Specific:** Your goal should be clear and detailed.
- **Measurable:** You must be able to track your progress.
- **Achievable:** It should challenge you but remain realistic.

- **Relevant:** Your goal must align with your larger financial vision.
- **Time-bound:** Set a deadline to create urgency and focus.

Examples of SMART Goals:

1. **Vague Goal:** "I want to save more money."

❖ **SMART Goal:** "I will save $5,000 for a down payment on a house by December 31st."

2. **Vague Goal:** "I want to get out of debt."

❖ **SMART Goal:** "I will pay off my $3,000 credit card balance within 12 months by allocating $250 monthly from my budget."

SMART goals turn abstract ideas into actionable plans, increasing your chances of success.

Differentiating Between Short-Term and Long-Term Goals

Not all financial goals are created equal. To stay organized and motivated, it's crucial to separate short-term goals from long-term ones.

Short-Term Goals (Less than 1 Year):

These are goals you can achieve relatively quickly. Examples include:

- Building an emergency fund.
- Paying off a small debt.
- Saving for a vacation.

Long-Term Goals (1 Year or More):

These are larger objectives that require time and consistent effort. Examples include:

- Saving for a down payment on a house.
- Investing for retirement.
- Funding a child's education.

By categorizing your goals, you'll know where to focus your energy and how to allocate your resources effectively.

Identifying Your "Why" for Financial Transformation

Your "why" is the emotional anchor behind your goals. It's what keeps you motivated when things get tough. Without a strong "why," it's easy to lose steam or revert to old habits.

Discovering Your Why:

- **Ask yourself:** What's the real reason I want financial freedom?

- To provide a better future for your family?
- To reduce stress and enjoy life more?
- To leave a legacy for future generations?

- **Write it down:** Keeping your "why" visible serves as a daily reminder of your purpose.

For example, if your goal is to save $10,000, your "why" might be to secure your child's education or prepare for unexpected emergencies. Having a deeply personal reason increases your commitment to the process.

Tools for Documenting and Tracking Your Progress

Once you've defined your goals, you'll need tools and systems to track your progress. Monitoring your achievements not only keeps you accountable but also provides motivation as you celebrate milestones.

Tools to Consider:

1. **Budgeting Apps:** Tools like Mint, YNAB (You Need A Budget), and EveryDollar can help you track income, expenses, and savings goals.
2. **Goal Trackers:** Apps like Strides or Habitica let you set and monitor financial objectives.
3. **Spreadsheets:** A simple Excel or Google Sheets document can be customized to suit your needs.
4. **Journals:** Writing in a financial journal allows for reflection and adjustment.

Actionable Steps:

- Set a specific day each week to review your progress.
- Celebrate small wins, such as saving an extra $50 or cutting an unnecessary expense.

➢ Adjust your goals as needed to stay realistic and motivated.

Tracking tools make your journey measurable and give you clarity about what's working and what needs adjustment.

Final Thoughts

Defining your wealth vision is the first and most crucial step on your path to financial freedom. It provides the clarity, focus, and motivation you need to take meaningful action. Remember, this is a process—it's okay if your goals evolve as your circumstances change.

By understanding the importance of financial goals, visualizing your ideal future, and creating actionable steps with SMART goals, you're laying a strong foundation for success. Keep your "why" at the forefront of your journey, and use tools to stay on track. Your wealth vision is more than just a dream—it's the blueprint for the life you're about to build. Let's move forward and start turning your vision into reality.

Chapter 02

Assessing Your Current Financial Reality

Before you can improve your finances, you need to understand where you stand today. Think of this chapter as a financial check-up. Just as you wouldn't skip a health assessment when starting a new fitness plan, you shouldn't avoid evaluating your current financial situation. This is the foundation for everything you'll build in the weeks ahead. By being honest and thorough, you'll gain clarity and uncover opportunities for growth.

Taking Inventory of Income, Expenses, Assets, and Liabilities

The first step in assessing your financial reality is to take inventory of four key components: income, expenses, assets, and liabilities.

1. Income:

- **What to include:** Your salary, side hustles, rental income, investment returns, and any other sources of money coming in regularly.
- **Actionable Step:** Create a list of all income streams, noting whether they're fixed (e.g., a salary) or variable (e.g., freelance work).

2. Expenses:

- **What to include:** Everything you spend money on, from rent/mortgage payments to groceries, entertainment, and subscriptions.

- **Actionable Step:** Review your bank statements and credit card bills for the past three months to capture a complete picture of your spending habits.

3. Assets:

- **What to include:** Things you own that have monetary value, such as cash savings, investments, property, vehicles, and valuable items.
- **Actionable Step:** List each asset and estimate its current value.

4. Liabilities:

- **What to include:** Debts and obligations, such as credit card balances, student loans, mortgages, car loans, and unpaid bills.
- **Actionable Step:** Write down each liability along with its outstanding balance, interest rate, and monthly payment.

Organize these details in a simple table or spreadsheet to give yourself a clear financial snapshot.

Understanding Your Net Worth and Why It Matters

Your **net worth** is the cornerstone of your financial health. It's the difference between what you own (assets) and what you owe (liabilities).

How to Calculate Net Worth:

$$\text{Net Worth} = \text{Total Assets} - \text{Total Liabilities}$$

- If your assets exceed your liabilities, you have a positive net worth.
- If your liabilities outweigh your assets, you have a negative net worth.

Why It Matters:

- **Measures Progress:** Tracking your net worth over time helps you see the results of your financial decisions.
- **Reveals Opportunities:** A negative net worth highlights areas where you need to focus, such as reducing debt or building savings.
- **Guides Goal Setting:** Understanding your starting point makes it easier to set realistic financial goals.

Actionable Step: Calculate your net worth today and commit to updating it monthly or quarterly. This regular check-in will keep you motivated and focused.

Identifying Financial Leaks in Your Budget

Even the most well-intentioned budgets can spring leaks. These are small, often unnoticed expenses that add up over time and drain your resources.

Common Financial Leaks:

- **Subscriptions:** Are you paying for streaming services or apps you no longer use?
- **Impulse Purchases:** Unplanned spending on small items can snowball quickly.
- **Overpaying for Services:** Review your insurance, utilities, and phone plans for potential savings.
- **Fees and Penalties:** Late payment fees or ATM charges can add up unnecessarily.

How to Fix Financial Leaks:

- **Audit Your Spending:** Review every expense and question its value.
- **Negotiate and Shop Around:** Call service providers to ask for discounts or switch to more affordable options.
- **Set Spending Limits:** Use cash envelopes or budgeting apps to control discretionary spending.

Actionable Step: Write down three expenses you can eliminate or reduce immediately and commit to acting on them this week.

Categorizing Expenses into "Needs," "Wants," and "Luxuries"

Not all expenses are created equal. Categorizing your spending helps you prioritize and make informed decisions.

Categories Defined:

1. **Needs:** Essential expenses required for survival or maintaining your basic standard of living. Examples: housing, utilities, groceries, and minimum debt payments.
2. **Wants:** Non-essential items that improve your quality of life but aren't strictly necessary. Examples: dining out, streaming subscriptions, and hobbies.
3. **Luxuries:** High-cost, non-essential items or experiences that are purely indulgent. Examples: designer goods, extravagant vacations, or top-tier car models.

Actionable Step:

Review your expenses and assign each one to a category. Ask yourself:

- Can this expense be reduced or eliminated?
- Does this expense align with my financial goals?

Pro Tip: Use the **50/30/20 Rule** as a guideline:

- 50% of your income goes toward needs.
- 30% goes toward wants.
- 20% goes toward savings and debt repayment.

Setting Benchmarks to Measure Improvement

Benchmarks are essential for tracking progress and staying motivated. They provide a reference point to measure success and guide your financial decisions.

How to Set Benchmarks:

1. **Emergency Fund:** Start with a goal of saving $1,000, then aim for 3-6 months of living expenses.
2. **Debt Reduction:** Set a target for paying off a specific percentage of your debt within six months.
3. **Savings Rate:** Aim to save at least 20% of your income, adjusting based on your circumstances.
4. **Spending Limit:** Reduce discretionary spending by a set percentage, such as cutting dining out by 25%.

Actionable Step: Choose one benchmark for each of the following categories: savings, debt, and spending. Write them down and create a timeline for achieving them.

The Importance of Honesty and Self-Assessment

Financial improvement starts with honesty. It's tempting to sugarcoat the numbers or ignore problem areas, but denial only delays progress.

Why Honesty Matters:

- **Clarity:** Knowing the truth about your finances helps you make informed decisions.
- **Empowerment:** Acknowledging your challenges puts you in control of addressing them.
- **Motivation:** Facing the facts can inspire you to take action and avoid repeating mistakes.

Actionable Step: Commit to being truthful with yourself. Write down one financial habit you've been avoiding or denying (e.g., overspending, not saving) and one action you can take today to address it.

Final Thoughts

Assessing your current financial reality isn't always easy, but it's a necessary step on the road to financial freedom. By taking inventory of your finances, calculating your net worth, identifying leaks, and categorizing your expenses, you'll gain a clear picture of where you stand. From this foundation, you can set meaningful benchmarks and begin making progress.

Remember, honesty is your greatest ally in this process. Facing the truth, even when it's uncomfortable, empowers you to take control and build a better financial future. The journey starts here—let's keep moving forward!

Chapter 03

Mastering the Wealth Mindset

Building wealth isn't just about numbers—it starts in your mind. Your thoughts, beliefs, and habits shape your financial outcomes more than you might realize. This chapter is dedicated to helping you cultivate a mindset that sets you up for long-term financial success. By breaking free from limiting beliefs, embracing a growth mindset, and practicing habits of abundance, you'll transform the way you approach money.

Breaking Free from Limiting Money Beliefs

Many people unknowingly hold onto beliefs about money that sabotage their success. These limiting beliefs often stem from upbringing, societal messages, or personal experiences.

Common Limiting Money Beliefs:

- "Money is the root of all evil."
- "Rich people are greedy or selfish."
- "I'm not good with money."
- "I'll never make enough to save or invest."

How to Overcome Limiting Beliefs:

1. **Identify Them:** Write down your negative thoughts about money. Awareness is the first step to change.
2. **Challenge Them:** Ask yourself if these beliefs are facts or opinions. For example, is it truly evil to desire financial security for your family?
3. **Reframe Them:** Replace negative beliefs with positive, empowering ones.

- ❖ Instead of "I'm not good with money," say, "I'm learning to manage money wisely."

Actionable Step:

Take five minutes today to write down one limiting belief and its positive replacement. Repeat this new belief to yourself every day.

Adopting a Growth Mindset for Wealth Building

A growth mindset is the belief that your abilities and intelligence can improve with effort and persistence. When applied to money, it means viewing financial challenges as opportunities to learn and grow.

Key Traits of a Wealth Growth Mindset:

- ➤ **Embraces Learning:** Invest time in understanding personal finance, even if it feels overwhelming at first.
- ➤ **Sees Failure as Feedback:** View financial mistakes as lessons, not setbacks.
- ➤ **Focuses on Possibility:** Believe that wealth-building is achievable, regardless of your starting point.

Practical Tips to Develop a Growth Mindset:

- ➤ Read books or listen to podcasts about personal finance.

- Seek out stories of individuals who've overcome financial challenges.
- Surround yourself with people who inspire you to grow financially.

Actionable Step: Identify one financial skill you want to improve (e.g., budgeting, investing) and commit to learning about it this week.

Cultivating Financial Discipline and Delayed Gratification

Discipline and the ability to delay gratification are essential for building wealth. They help you stay focused on long-term goals instead of succumbing to short-term temptations.

Why Delayed Gratification Matters:

- It allows you to save and invest instead of overspending on fleeting pleasures.
- It builds habits that compound your wealth over time.

Practical Strategies to Develop Financial Discipline:

1. **Create a Spending Pause Rule:** Wait 24-48 hours before making non-essential purchases.
2. **Automate Savings:** Set up automatic transfers to your savings or investment accounts to remove temptation.

3. **Set Micro-Goals:** Break larger financial goals into smaller, achievable milestones to stay motivated.

Actionable Step: Choose one expense you can delay or eliminate this week. Redirect that money toward your financial goals.

Practicing Gratitude and Abundance Thinking

Gratitude and abundance thinking shift your focus from scarcity ("I'll never have enough") to appreciation for what you already have. This mindset encourages positive financial behavior and attracts opportunities.

Benefits of Gratitude:

- Reduces financial stress by focusing on the present.
- Helps you recognize and maximize the resources you already have.

How to Practice Gratitude Daily:

- Write down three things you're grateful for related to money or resources.

❖ Example: "I'm thankful for my job, my health, and the ability to save money."

- Take time to appreciate small financial wins, like paying off a credit card or sticking to your budget.

Actionable Step: Start a gratitude journal specifically for finances. Each day, write one thing you're grateful for about your financial situation.

Surrounding Yourself with Financially Motivated Influences

Your environment plays a significant role in shaping your mindset. Surrounding yourself with people and resources that align with your financial goals can help you stay motivated.

Who to Surround Yourself With:

- **Mentors:** Seek guidance from people who've achieved the financial success you desire.
- **Like-Minded Peers:** Join communities, clubs, or online groups focused on financial growth.
- **Educators:** Follow personal finance experts who provide actionable advice.

Avoid Negative Influences:

- Steer clear of individuals or groups that encourage reckless spending or negativity about money.

Actionable Step: Identify one positive financial influence to connect with this week, whether it's joining a group, following a finance expert, or reaching out to a mentor.

Daily Affirmations to Strengthen Your Financial Habits

Affirmations are powerful statements that reinforce positive beliefs and behaviors. They help you stay focused on your goals and build confidence in your ability to succeed financially.

Examples of Financial Affirmations:

- ➢ "I am capable of achieving my financial goals."
- ➢ "Money flows to me effortlessly and abundantly."
- ➢ "I make wise financial decisions every day."

How to Use Affirmations:

- ➢ Write them down and place them where you'll see them daily (e.g., on your mirror, computer, or phone).
- ➢ Say them aloud each morning to start your day with a positive mindset.

Actionable Step: Create three personal financial affirmations today and commit to repeating them every morning.

Final Thoughts

Mastering the wealth mindset is about more than just thinking positively—it's about transforming the way you view, approach, and handle money. By breaking free from limiting beliefs, embracing a growth mindset, and practicing gratitude, you lay the psychological groundwork for financial success.

Remember, your mindset is your most powerful financial tool. It influences your actions, decisions, and ultimately, your outcomes. Commit to cultivating a mindset that supports your goals, and you'll find that the habits of wealth-building become second nature. Let's take this newfound mindset into the next steps of your financial journey.

PART 2: Taking Control of Your Finances

Chapter 04
Building an Effective Budget

Creating wealth begins with mastering one of the most fundamental financial skills: budgeting. A budget isn't just a list of expenses; it's your financial roadmap, guiding every dollar toward your goals. In this chapter, you'll learn how to build an effective budget tailored to your needs and lifestyle. By choosing the right method, leveraging technology, and practicing regular reviews, you'll gain control over your finances and make consistent progress toward wealth creation.

Understanding the Role of Budgeting in Wealth Creation

Budgeting is often misunderstood as restrictive, but it's actually empowering. A budget doesn't limit your freedom; it creates clarity and control over your money.

Why Budgeting is Essential for Wealth:

- ➢ **Prioritization:** A budget ensures your money aligns with your goals, not impulsive spending.
- ➢ **Awareness:** It helps you understand where your money goes, so you can identify areas for improvement.
- ➢ **Discipline:** Regular budgeting builds habits of intentional spending and saving.
- ➢ **Growth:** When you control your money, you can direct more toward savings, investments, and wealth-building opportunities.

Actionable Step: Reflect on one financial goal (e.g., saving for a home or paying off debt). Use this goal as motivation to commit to budgeting.

Choosing a Budgeting Method

There's no one-size-fits-all approach to budgeting. The best method is the one that fits your lifestyle and encourages consistency.

Popular Budgeting Methods:

Zero-Based Budgeting:

- ❖ Every dollar has a job. Assign your income to expenses, savings, and debt until you reach zero.
- ❖ Great for: Detailed planners who want full control over their finances.

50/30/20 Rule:

- ❖ Allocate 50% of your income to needs, 30% to wants, and 20% to savings or debt repayment.
- ❖ Great for: Beginners or those seeking a simple structure.

Pay-Yourself-First Budgeting:

- ❖ Prioritize savings and investments before allocating money to expenses.
- ❖ Great for: Savers focused on long-term wealth.

Envelope System:

- ❖ Divide cash into envelopes for specific spending categories. Stop spending once the envelope is empty.
- ❖ Great for: Those struggling with overspending or managing discretionary expenses.

Actionable Step: Choose one budgeting method to try this month. Test its effectiveness and adjust as needed.

Automating Savings and Expense Tracking

Automation simplifies budgeting by removing the temptation to spend money before saving it. It also streamlines tracking, so you don't need to monitor every dollar manually.

Benefits of Automation:

- ➤ Ensures consistency in saving and paying bills.
- ➤ Reduces the mental load of financial management.
- ➤ Helps avoid late fees or missed payments.

How to Automate Your Budget:

1. **Set Up Direct Deposit Splits:** Allocate a portion of your paycheck to savings or investments automatically.
2. **Use Auto-Pay for Bills:** Schedule recurring payments for fixed expenses like rent, utilities, and loans.
3. **Link Expense-Tracking Apps:** Sync your bank accounts with apps that categorize your spending (e.g., Mint, YNAB, or Personal Capital).

Actionable Step: Automate one financial process today, such as transferring a percentage of your income to savings.

Adjusting Your Budget for Variable Income or Unexpected Expenses

Life is unpredictable, and so is your income or expense flow. A flexible budget adapts to these changes without derailing your goals.

How to Handle Variable Income:

- **Set a Baseline Budget:** Base your budget on the lowest expected monthly income.
- **Create a Buffer Fund:** Save extra income during high-earning months to cover shortfalls in leaner ones.
- **Prioritize Essentials:** Focus on fixed expenses and necessities before allocating money to wants.

Managing Unexpected Expenses:

- **Emergency Fund:** Build and maintain 3-6 months' worth of expenses for unforeseen costs.
- **Review and Reallocate:** Adjust non-essential categories to cover the unexpected expense temporarily.
- **Separate "Wants" from Emergencies:** Avoid using emergency funds for discretionary spending.

Actionable Step: Start an emergency fund if you don't already have one. Aim to set aside at least $500 as a starting point.

Tools and Apps for Effortless Budgeting

Technology has made budgeting more accessible than ever. The right tools can help you stay organized, track spending, and make adjustments on the go.

Top Budgeting Tools and Apps:

1. **Mint:** Tracks expenses, categorizes spending, and provides a complete financial overview.
2. **YNAB (You Need a Budget):** Encourages proactive budgeting and assigning every dollar a purpose.
3. **Personal Capital:** Focuses on both budgeting and wealth-building through investment tracking.
4. **Goodbudget:** A digital take on the envelope system.
5. **Spreadsheets:** For those who prefer a custom approach, create a simple Excel or Google Sheets budget.

Actionable Step: Download and explore one budgeting app this week. Test its features to see if it fits your needs.

Monthly Review Strategies to Stay on Track

Budgeting isn't a one-and-done activity. Regular reviews ensure you're staying aligned with your goals and making progress.

How to Conduct a Monthly Budget Review:

1. **Compare Budget vs. Actual:** Identify discrepancies between your planned and actual spending.
2. **Evaluate Progress:** Measure how well you're advancing toward your financial goals.
3. **Adjust for Changes:** Update your budget for any new expenses or income fluctuations.
4. **Celebrate Wins:** Acknowledge and reward yourself for sticking to your budget.

Questions to Ask During Your Review:

➢ Did I stay within my budgeted amounts?
➢ What categories exceeded my expectations?
➢ How can I improve next month?

Actionable Step: Schedule a recurring date for your monthly budget review. Make it a non-negotiable appointment.

Final Thoughts

Building an effective budget is one of the most empowering steps in your financial journey. By choosing the right method, automating processes, and conducting regular reviews, you'll develop habits that keep you on track toward wealth creation.

Budgeting isn't about deprivation—it's about taking control of your money so you can achieve your dreams. With your budget in place, you're ready to tackle the next chapter in your journey: managing debt effectively.

Chapter 05

Slashing Debt the Smart Way

Debt can feel like a heavy weight, but with the right strategies, you can free yourself and redirect that money toward building wealth. This chapter will guide you through understanding the true cost of debt, choosing the most effective repayment method, and adopting habits to stay debt-free. By breaking it down into manageable steps, you'll learn how to tackle debt with confidence and clarity.

Understanding the True Cost of Debt

Debt isn't just about the amount you owe; it's about how much it costs over time. Understanding the true cost of debt can motivate you to prioritize repayment.

The Impact of Interest Rates:

- ➤ High-interest debt, such as credit cards, can double or triple the amount you owe if left unpaid.
- ➤ Compound interest works against you with debt, increasing the total cost exponentially over time.

Calculating the Total Cost of Debt:

1. Review your debts, including the principal amount, interest rates, and minimum payments.
2. Use an online debt calculator to see how much you'll pay over time if you stick to the minimum payments.

Real-World Example:

- A $5,000 credit card debt at a 20% interest rate can take 30 years to pay off if you only make minimum payments—and cost you over $12,000 in total.

Actionable Step: List all your debts, including balances, interest rates, and minimum payments. Calculate the total cost if left unpaid.

Comparing Popular Debt Repayment Methods: Snowball vs. Avalanche

Choosing the right repayment strategy can make all the difference in your journey to becoming debt-free.

Snowball Method:

- Pay off the smallest debts first while making minimum payments on larger debts.
- Benefits: Quick wins boost motivation and confidence.
- Example: If you have debts of $500, $2,000, and $10,000, you'd focus on the $500 debt first.

Avalanche Method:

- Focus on paying off debts with the highest interest rates first.
- Benefits: Saves money in the long term by reducing interest paid.
- Example: If you have a credit card at 18% interest and a car loan at 5%, prioritize the credit card.

Which Method Should You Choose?

- **Snowball Method:** Best if you need psychological wins to stay motivated.
- **Avalanche Method:** Best if you're disciplined and want to minimize overall cost.

Actionable Step: Choose a repayment method and list your debts in the order you'll tackle them.

Prioritizing High-Interest Debts

High-interest debts are the biggest drain on your finances. Prioritizing them ensures you stop wasting money on excessive interest payments.

Steps to Tackle High-Interest Debts:

1. Identify all debts with interest rates above 10%.
2. Focus on paying more than the minimum for these debts while maintaining minimum payments on others.
3. Consider transferring high-interest debt to a lower-interest option, such as a balance transfer card or personal loan, if feasible.

Actionable Step: Highlight your debts with the highest interest rates and create a plan to address them first.

Strategies for Negotiating with Creditors or Consolidating Debt

Sometimes, negotiating or consolidating your debts can make repayment more manageable and save you money.

Negotiating with Creditors:

- **Request Lower Interest Rates:** Call your credit card company and ask for a rate reduction. Explain your situation and payment history.
- **Settle for Less:** If you have a lump sum, some creditors may accept a smaller payment to close the account.
- **Hardship Plans:** Many lenders offer temporary relief programs for those facing financial difficulties.

Debt Consolidation Options:

- **Balance Transfer Cards:** Move high-interest credit card debt to a card with a low or 0% introductory APR.
- **Personal Loans:** Use a fixed-rate loan to consolidate multiple debts into one payment.
- **Home Equity Loans:** Tap into home equity for a lower-interest loan, but be cautious as your home is collateral.

Actionable Step: Contact one creditor to explore options for reducing interest rates or consolidating debt.

The Importance of Avoiding New Debt During Repayment

Repaying debt while accumulating more is like trying to fill a bucket with a hole in it. To break free, you must stop adding to your debt load.

Strategies to Avoid New Debt:

1. **Freeze Credit Cards:** Place them in a drawer — or even a block of ice — while focusing on repayment.
2. **Adopt a Cash-Only Approach:** Use cash or a debit card for all purchases to prevent overspending.
3. **Build an Emergency Fund:** Start with a small fund ($500–$1,000) to cover unexpected expenses without relying on credit.
4. **Set Spending Rules:** Limit discretionary spending until your debt is under control.

Actionable Step: Commit to using only cash or debit for non-essential expenses this month.

Celebrating Milestones in Your Debt-Free Journey

Repaying debt is a significant achievement, and celebrating milestones along the way keeps you motivated.

Why Celebrate Small Wins?

- It reinforces positive behavior and keeps you engaged in the process.
- It makes the journey feel less overwhelming.

Ideas for Celebrating Debt Milestones:

- **Small Debts Paid Off:** Treat yourself to a low-cost reward, like a favorite meal.

- **Major Debt Eliminated:** Plan a day trip or experience that doesn't involve taking on new debt.
- **Debt-Free Status:** Celebrate big! Host a debt-free party or invest in something meaningful for your future.

Actionable Step: Choose one way to celebrate your next debt milestone and plan for it in advance.

Final Thoughts

Slashing debt isn't just about numbers—it's about reclaiming your financial freedom. By understanding the true cost of debt, choosing a repayment strategy, and avoiding new debt, you'll make steady progress toward your goals. Remember, each payment brings you closer to financial independence.

Stay focused, celebrate your victories, and use the momentum from this chapter to propel yourself into the next phase of your financial journey. With your debt under control, you'll have the tools to start saving and investing for the future.

Chapter 06
Establishing a Financial Safety Net

Building wealth is impossible without first establishing a financial safety net. Life is full of uncertainties, and emergencies can derail even the most solid financial plans. This chapter will guide you through the importance of an emergency fund, how to build one, and other protective measures to shield your wealth.

Why Emergency Funds Are Critical for Wealth Building

An emergency fund serves as your financial buffer, protecting you from unexpected expenses that could force you into debt or disrupt your long-term goals.

Key Benefits of an Emergency Fund:

- **Debt Prevention:** Prevents reliance on credit cards or loans during unexpected situations.
- **Peace of Mind:** Reduces financial stress and allows you to focus on building wealth.
- **Flexibility:** Provides the freedom to make better financial decisions during tough times.

Real-Life Example: Imagine losing your job unexpectedly. An emergency fund can cover your expenses until you find a new one, preventing financial panic or poor decisions like selling investments prematurely.

Actionable Step: Reflect on recent emergencies and how an emergency fund could have helped. Use this as motivation to start saving.

Determining the Right Amount to Save for Emergencies

The ideal size of an emergency fund varies depending on your financial situation, lifestyle, and responsibilities.

How Much Do You Need?

- **General Rule of Thumb:** Save 3-6 months of essential living expenses.
- **Single vs. Dual Income Households:** If you're single or your household relies on one income, aim closer to 6 months.
- **Variable Income:** If your income fluctuates, like freelancers or business owners, consider saving 9-12 months of expenses.

Steps to Calculate Your Target:

1. List your essential monthly expenses, such as rent, utilities, groceries, and insurance.
2. Multiply this amount by the number of months you want to cover.

Example: If your monthly expenses are $3,000, a 6-month fund would total $18,000.

Actionable Step: Calculate your emergency fund target based on your current monthly expenses.

Finding Creative Ways to Build Your Emergency Fund

Saving for emergencies may seem daunting, but with a clear plan and creativity, you can start building your fund today.

Simple Strategies to Jumpstart Your Savings:

- **Set a Dedicated Savings Goal:** Open a separate savings account for emergencies and automate monthly contributions.
- **Redirect Windfalls:** Use tax refunds, bonuses, or unexpected income to boost your fund.
- **Sell Unused Items:** Declutter your home and sell items online or at a garage sale.
- **Temporary Spending Freeze:** Commit to a no-spend month and redirect those savings to your fund.

Boosting Savings Without Sacrificing Essentials:

- **Negotiate Bills:** Call service providers for discounts on cable, internet, or insurance.
- **Cut Small Luxuries:** Skip daily coffee shop visits or dining out for a few months.
- **Side Hustles:** Consider freelance work, tutoring, or part-time gigs to earn extra income.

Actionable Step: Choose one creative method to start building your emergency fund this week.

Where to Store Your Emergency Savings

Your emergency fund should be easily accessible, but also separate from your day-to-day spending to avoid temptation.

Best Places to Store Your Fund:

- **High-Yield Savings Accounts:** These accounts offer safety and a small return on your savings.
- **Money Market Accounts:** A mix of higher interest rates and check-writing capabilities for emergencies.
- **Certificates of Deposit (CDs):** Consider short-term CDs with no penalties for early withdrawal if you want to lock in a slightly higher rate.

Places to Avoid:

- **Stocks or Investments:** These carry risk and may not be easily accessible during emergencies.
- **Under Your Mattress:** Keeping cash at home isn't secure or practical.

Actionable Step: Open a dedicated high-yield savings account for your emergency fund if you don't already have one.

The Role of Insurance in Protecting Your Wealth

While an emergency fund helps with unexpected costs, insurance provides an additional layer of protection for major financial setbacks.

Types of Insurance to Consider:

1. **Health Insurance:** Covers medical emergencies and prevents high out-of-pocket costs.
2. **Homeowners or Renters Insurance:** Protects your home and belongings from damage or theft.
3. **Auto Insurance:** Ensures financial protection in case of accidents or vehicle damage.
4. **Disability Insurance:** Replaces income if you're unable to work due to illness or injury.
5. **Life Insurance:** Provides financial security for your loved ones if you pass away.

Balancing Insurance and Savings:

- Use insurance for large, catastrophic risks (e.g., medical emergencies).
- Rely on your emergency fund for smaller, short-term expenses (e.g., car repairs).

Actionable Step: Review your current insurance policies to ensure adequate coverage for your needs.

Evaluating and Adjusting Your Safety Net Periodically

Your emergency fund and safety measures should evolve as your financial situation changes.

When to Reassess Your Safety Net:

- ➢ **Life Changes:** Adjust for major events like marriage, having children, or changing jobs.
- ➢ **Inflation:** Review your fund annually to ensure it keeps pace with rising costs.
- ➢ **New Goals:** Update your savings target if your lifestyle or financial goals shift.

How to Stay on Track:

- ➢ Schedule a quarterly financial check-up to evaluate your progress.
- ➢ Adjust your contributions if you experience a raise or reduction in income.

Actionable Step: Set a reminder to review your emergency fund and insurance policies every six months.

Final Thoughts

Establishing a financial safety net is a foundational step in building wealth. Your emergency fund provides peace of mind, prevents debt, and allows you to focus on long-term goals. Coupled with adequate insurance and regular adjustments, your safety net will keep you protected from life's uncertainties.

By committing to the strategies outlined in this chapter, you're creating a solid financial shield that enables you to face challenges with confidence and resilience. Your safety net isn't just a financial tool—it's a key to unlocking a stable and prosperous future.

Part 3: Growing and Protecting Your Wealth

Chapter 07
Mastering the Basics of Investing

Investing is the gateway to building wealth that grows beyond your immediate efforts. While saving money is essential, it's investing that truly unlocks financial freedom by leveraging the power of compound interest and long-term growth. This chapter will guide you through the foundational concepts of investing and how to set yourself up for success.

Understanding Compound Interest and Its Power

Compound interest is the foundation of wealth creation. It's the process where your investments earn interest, and that interest earns even more interest over time.

Why Compound Interest Matters:

- **Exponential Growth:** Small investments made consistently can grow significantly over time.
- **The Earlier, the Better:** Starting early allows your money more time to compound.
- **Hands-Off Wealth Building:** Once set up, compounding works for you without constant effort.

Example of Compound Interest:

- If you invest $5,000 annually at an average return of 7%, you'll have over $500,000 in 30 years.
- If you wait 10 years to start, you'll have less than $250,000.

Actionable Step: Use a compound interest calculator to see how your savings can grow over time, motivating you to start investing immediately.

Overview of Investment Types

Understanding different investment types allows you to diversify your portfolio and manage risk effectively.

Common Investment Options:

1. **Stocks:** Ownership in a company, offering high returns with higher risk.
2. **Bonds:** Loans to companies or governments, providing lower risk and steady returns.
3. **Real Estate:** Investing in property for rental income or value appreciation.
4. **Mutual Funds and ETFs:** Pooled investments managed by professionals, offering diversification.
5. **Savings and Certificates of Deposit (CDs):** Low-risk options with modest returns, ideal for short-term goals.

Diversification:

- Diversification spreads your investments across different asset types to reduce risk.
- Example: A mix of stocks for growth, bonds for stability, and real estate for consistent income.

Actionable Step: Research one type of investment that aligns with your goals and begin exploring how to start.

Determining Your Risk Tolerance and Investment Strategy

Risk tolerance reflects your ability and willingness to endure market ups and downs.

How to Assess Your Risk Tolerance:

- **Time Horizon:** The longer you plan to invest, the more risk you can afford.
- **Financial Situation:** If you have a strong safety net, you may take on more risk.
- **Emotional Comfort:** Can you handle market fluctuations without panic selling?

Creating an Investment Strategy:

- **Conservative:** Focus on bonds and stable assets with lower returns but less volatility.
- **Balanced:** A mix of stocks and bonds for moderate growth and stability.
- **Aggressive:** Prioritize high-growth stocks, suitable for younger investors with long-term horizons.

Actionable Step: Take an online risk tolerance quiz or consult a financial advisor to determine your investment style.

Setting Up Retirement Accounts

Retirement accounts are tax-advantaged tools that help you save and grow your wealth for the future.

Types of Retirement Accounts:

1. **401(k):** Employer-sponsored plans with tax-deferred growth. Many employers offer matching contributions, which is essentially free money.
2. **Traditional IRA:** Tax-deferred individual retirement account with annual contribution limits.
3. **Roth IRA:** Contributions are taxed upfront, but withdrawals in retirement are tax-free.
4. **SEP IRA or Solo 401(k):** Retirement accounts designed for self-employed individuals.

Maximizing Contributions:

- Contribute enough to your 401(k) to get the full employer match.
- Aim to max out your IRA contributions annually.
- Automate contributions to stay consistent.

Actionable Step: Open an IRA or review your 401(k) options and ensure you're maximizing your benefits.

Avoiding Common Investing Pitfalls

Investing mistakes can cost you time, money, and confidence. Recognizing and avoiding these pitfalls ensures smoother growth.

Common Mistakes to Avoid:

- **Timing the Market:** Trying to predict market highs and lows often leads to losses.
- **Neglecting Diversification:** Putting all your money into one investment increases risk.
- **Overreacting to Market Changes:** Emotional decisions can result in panic selling.
- **Ignoring Fees:** High fees on investments or advisors can erode returns over time.
- **Failing to Reinvest Dividends:** Reinvesting dividends boosts your compounding growth.

Actionable Step: Create a written investing plan to guide decisions and prevent emotional reactions.

Leveraging Professional Advice and Resources

You don't have to navigate the world of investing alone. Leveraging expert advice can accelerate your success.

Ways to Access Expert Guidance:

1. **Financial Advisors:** Choose a fiduciary advisor who prioritizes your interests.
2. **Robo-Advisors:** Low-cost, automated platforms that create and manage portfolios.
3. **Books and Courses:** Educate yourself through reputable investing resources.
4. **Community Groups:** Join investing groups or forums to share knowledge and strategies.

Benefits of Seeking Help:

- Professionals can help you tailor strategies to your goals.
- Advisors and robo-advisors simplify complex decisions like tax optimization.

Actionable Step: Schedule a consultation with a financial advisor or explore a robo-advisor platform to get started.

Final Thoughts

Mastering the basics of investing is a crucial step in your journey to financial independence. By understanding the power of compound interest, choosing investments wisely, and avoiding common pitfalls, you're setting yourself up for sustainable growth.

Investing isn't just about money—it's about creating opportunities for your future self. Every dollar you invest today is a step closer to the life you envision. Take that step now, and let your money start working for you.

Chapter 08

Increasing Your Income Streams

One of the most powerful strategies for building lasting wealth is increasing your income streams. Relying solely on a single paycheck can limit your financial growth, but diversifying your sources of income provides stability, flexibility, and an opportunity for faster wealth accumulation. This chapter will guide you through practical ways to grow your primary income, explore side hustles, invest in yourself, and create passive income streams.

Identifying Opportunities to Grow Your Primary Income

Before seeking additional income sources, it's important to first explore opportunities to increase your primary income. This approach ensures you're maximizing what you already have before diversifying.

Ways to Grow Your Primary Income:

Request a Raise or Promotion:

1. Do you feel your work is undervalued? Build a strong case for a raise or promotion by documenting your achievements, impact, and market salary comparisons.
2. Prepare for a discussion with your boss by articulating your contributions and presenting data showing how your work has positively impacted the company.

Seek Career Advancement or Lateral Moves:

- If your current position has limited growth opportunities, consider pursuing a promotion or lateral move within your company.
- Research the skills and qualifications required for advancement and set a goal to meet them.

Change Employers for a Higher Salary:

- Sometimes, the best way to increase income is to switch jobs. Job-hopping can often lead to higher salary increases compared to staying in the same company for years.
- Be strategic in evaluating companies that offer better pay, benefits, and career growth.

Improve Your Negotiation Skills:

- Whether negotiating salary, benefits, or a contract, honing your negotiation skills can significantly increase your income.
- Practice negotiation techniques and educate yourself on salary ranges in your field.

Actionable Step: Research salary trends for your current role and identify opportunities within your organization to increase your pay or responsibilities.

Exploring Side Hustles and Freelance Opportunities

Side hustles and freelancing are great ways to add extra income, diversify your earnings, and discover new passions. These opportunities can become significant contributors to your wealth-building strategy.

Popular Side Hustles to Consider:

Freelance Writing or Graphic Design:

1. If you have writing, graphic design, or web development skills, freelancing platforms like Upwork, Fiverr, or Freelancer offer access to clients seeking your expertise.
2. Start by creating a portfolio and bidding on smaller projects to build your reputation.

Rideshare Driving or Delivery:

- Apps like Uber, Lyft, DoorDash, and Postmates allow you to earn money with flexible hours.
- This is a great option for those with a car and a flexible schedule, and it requires minimal startup costs.

Online Tutoring or Teaching:

- If you're knowledgeable in a subject or language, consider tutoring students online via platforms like Chegg, Tutor.com, or VIPKid.
- You can set your own hours and work with students from around the world.

Social Media Management or Virtual Assistance:

- Many small businesses and entrepreneurs need help with managing social media accounts, handling customer inquiries, or administrative tasks.

- Virtual assistance is in high demand, and platforms like Zirtual or Belay can connect you with clients.

How to Get Started:

- Assess your skills and interests to find a side hustle that complements your main job.
- Start small, testing the waters before scaling up.
- Use online platforms to market yourself and connect with potential clients or employers.

Actionable Step: Identify one side hustle that interests you and begin researching platforms or opportunities in that field.

Investing in Skills and Education for Career Advancement

One of the best ways to increase your earning potential is by investing in your education and skills. In today's fast-changing world, continuous learning ensures you stay competitive and can advance in your career.

Key Areas to Focus On:

Industry-Specific Certifications:

- Some fields, such as tech, healthcare, and finance, reward employees who have specific certifications (e.g., PMP, CFA, coding boot camps).
- These certifications can increase your earning potential and make you more marketable.

Online Courses and Degrees:

- Websites like Coursera, Udemy, and LinkedIn Learning offer affordable courses that can help you gain new skills.
- Consider investing in a formal degree or certification if it aligns with your career goals.

Networking and Mentorship:

- Building relationships within your industry can lead to new opportunities, mentorship, and career growth.
- Attend conferences, webinars, and networking events to meet people who can guide your career path.

Soft Skills Development:

- Skills such as communication, leadership, negotiation, and time management are invaluable and can increase your value in any profession.
- Read books, take courses, or seek feedback to continually improve these areas.

Actionable Step: Research skills or certifications that can help you advance in your career and commit to learning at least one new skill this month.

Building Passive Income Streams (Dividends, Rental Income, etc.)

Passive income is money earned with minimal effort on your part after the initial setup. Building passive income streams is an essential strategy for long-term wealth building.

Types of Passive Income Streams:

Dividend Stocks:

- Dividend stocks pay you regular income in the form of dividends while allowing your investment to grow.
- Look for stocks with a strong history of paying dividends and consider reinvesting those dividends to boost growth.

Rental Properties:

- Buying and renting out property can provide steady cash flow.
- Real estate investment trusts (REITs) are also an option if you prefer to invest in property without owning it directly.

Peer-to-Peer Lending:

- Platforms like LendingClub allow you to lend money to individuals in exchange for interest payments.
- This is a higher-risk option, but it offers the potential for attractive returns.

Creating Digital Products:

- If you have knowledge in a particular field, consider creating eBooks, online courses, or stock photography that you can sell repeatedly.
- This requires an upfront investment of time or money, but once created, the products can generate passive income.

How to Get Started:

- Begin by researching the passive income streams that best align with your resources and interests.
- Start small and scale up as you become more comfortable with your chosen method.

Actionable Step: Choose one passive income stream to explore and take the first steps to get started.

Turning Hobbies into Profitable Ventures

Many people have hobbies or interests that can be monetized into profitable ventures. Turning your passion into income allows you to enjoy the process while earning money.

Examples of Monetizable Hobbies:

Photography:

- Sell your photos on stock photo websites or offer portrait or event photography services.
- Build a portfolio and market your services through social media or a personal website.

Crafting or Art:

- Platforms like Etsy provide an opportunity to sell handmade items such as jewelry, clothing, art, or home décor.
- Build a brand around your creations and use social media to promote your work.

Cooking or Baking:

- If you're skilled in the kitchen, consider catering, baking for special events, or offering cooking classes.
- Share recipes or start a food blog or YouTube channel to monetize your cooking passion.

Fitness or Wellness:

- Turn your fitness routine into a business by becoming a personal trainer, offering online fitness courses, or selling fitness equipment.
- Use social media to build a following and promote your services.

Actionable Step: Identify a hobby you're passionate about and explore how it can be monetized.

Avoiding Burnout While Pursuing Multiple Income Streams

While having multiple income streams is a great way to accelerate your wealth-building journey, it's important to avoid burnout.

Tips for Balancing Multiple Income Streams:

Set Realistic Goals:

- Prioritize your energy and resources by setting clear, achievable goals for each income stream.
- Avoid spreading yourself too thin by focusing on one or two streams at a time.

Time Management:

- ❖ Block out specific times in your week dedicated to each side hustle or business.
- ❖ Use tools like time-tracking apps or planners to stay organized and maintain a healthy work-life balance.

Outsource Tasks:

- ❖ For non-essential tasks, consider outsourcing them to save time and focus on what matters most.
- ❖ Hiring help can prevent you from feeling overwhelmed and allow you to scale more efficiently.

Actionable Step: Evaluate your current workload and identify ways to streamline or delegate tasks to maintain a sustainable balance.

Final Thoughts

Increasing your income streams is a powerful way to achieve financial freedom and accelerate wealth-building. By diversifying your sources of income—whether through career growth, side hustles, investments, or monetizing hobbies—you create a financial cushion that provides stability and growth opportunities.

Remember to start small, stay consistent, and avoid burnout by managing your time and energy effectively. With dedication, you can create multiple income streams that lead to long-term wealth and security.

Chapter 09
Protecting Your Wealth from Risks

Building wealth is an important goal, but equally important is protecting that wealth from various risks that could derail your financial progress. While many focus on increasing their income and investments, safeguarding your wealth is just as crucial for long-term financial security. In this chapter, we'll explore the key strategies for identifying, mitigating, and protecting your wealth from potential risks, both expected and unforeseen.

Identifying and Mitigating Financial Risks

Financial risks come in many forms, and some are more predictable than others. However, being proactive and identifying these risks allows you to take steps to minimize their impact.

Types of Financial Risks:

Market Risk

This involves fluctuations in the market, including stock market volatility and economic downturns. While you can't control the market, you can take steps to reduce your exposure through diversification and risk management strategies.

Credit Risk

If you rely on credit for purchases or investments, you're exposed to the risk of falling behind on payments or defaulting. This can damage your credit score and lead to higher borrowing costs. Mitigating credit risk requires maintaining a budget, paying off debts, and improving your credit score over time.

Inflation Risk

Inflation erodes the purchasing power of your money. It's important to invest in assets that outpace inflation (like stocks or real estate) to preserve your wealth over time.

Liquidity Risk

This risk arises when you can't quickly convert your assets into cash without a significant loss in value. Liquidity is especially important in times of financial emergencies, so it's crucial to keep an emergency fund or highly liquid investments that you can access when necessary.

Mitigating Financial Risks:

- **Diversify Your Investments**: Spreading your investments across various asset classes (stocks, bonds, real estate, etc.) reduces the risk of a total loss.
- **Regular Risk Assessments**: Continuously evaluate your financial portfolio to ensure it matches your risk tolerance and long-term goals.
- **Emergency Fund**: Building an emergency fund equal to at least three to six months of expenses can protect you in case of unexpected financial challenges.

Actionable Step: Review your current financial situation and identify the major risks you face. Take steps to mitigate those risks, such as diversifying investments or increasing your emergency fund.

Reviewing and Optimizing Your Insurance Coverage

Insurance is one of the most effective ways to protect your wealth from unexpected expenses. Without adequate insurance, you could face massive financial burdens that derail your wealth-building plans.

Types of Insurance to Consider:

Health Insurance

- Medical expenses can quickly drain your savings. Make sure you have comprehensive health insurance that covers both routine and emergency medical needs.
- Review your policy annually to ensure it meets your needs, especially if your health or family situation changes.

Life Insurance

- If you have dependents, life insurance is essential for ensuring they are financially supported in case of your unexpected death.
- The amount of coverage should be based on your family's needs, including current debts, living expenses, and future education costs.

Disability Insurance

- If you become ill or injured and can't work, disability insurance provides income replacement.
- Depending on your occupation and risk level, you may want to explore both short-term and long-term disability coverage.

Homeowners or Renters Insurance

- Protect your home, belongings, and liability against loss or damage.
- Review your policy regularly, especially after acquiring high-value items or making home improvements, to ensure adequate coverage.

Umbrella Insurance

- Umbrella policies provide additional liability coverage beyond your home and auto insurance. This is especially useful if you're at risk of large lawsuits or own significant assets.

Optimizing Your Insurance:

- **Compare Policies**: Don't settle for the first insurance policy you come across. Shop around and compare rates, benefits, and coverage options from different providers.
- **Increase Deductibles**: In some cases, increasing your deductible can reduce your monthly premiums, saving you money in the long run.

- **Regularly Update Coverage**: As your life situation changes, so should your insurance coverage. Update your policies to reflect any major life changes (e.g., marriage, buying a house, or starting a family).

Actionable Step: Review your insurance policies to ensure they cover all the essential areas. Make any adjustments necessary to optimize your coverage while minimizing costs.

Diversifying Investments to Reduce Risk Exposure

While it's important to accumulate wealth, it's equally important to spread your investments across a range of asset classes to mitigate risk. Diversification helps protect you from market volatility and ensures your investments remain resilient against various economic conditions.

The Importance of Diversification:

Reduces Volatility

- Diversifying your investments across different asset types (stocks, bonds, real estate, etc.) can reduce the overall volatility of your portfolio. While one asset class may be underperforming, others may be thriving, balancing the overall risk.

Protects Against Market Downturns

- Diversified portfolios are better equipped to weather market downturns. If stocks are taking a hit, bonds or real estate might be performing better.
- This balance ensures that you don't put all your financial eggs in one basket, reducing the risk of significant losses.

Increases Long-Term Stability

- A diversified portfolio can provide a more stable and reliable stream of returns over time. This stability is key to long-term wealth-building, as it ensures you're not overly exposed to short-term market fluctuations.

Strategies for Diversification:

- **Asset Allocation**: Divide your investments between different types of assets (stocks, bonds, real estate, commodities, etc.) based on your risk tolerance and financial goals.
- **Geographic Diversification**: Invest in both domestic and international markets to protect against country-specific risks.
- **Investment Vehicles**: Use mutual funds, exchange-traded funds (ETFs), or index funds to gain broad exposure to various sectors and industries.

Actionable Step: Reevaluate your investment portfolio and ensure it is properly diversified across multiple asset classes to reduce exposure to any one risk.

Preparing for Life Transitions (Marriage, Children, Retirement)

Life transitions are inevitable, and each one presents unique financial risks and opportunities. Being proactive in preparing for these transitions will help safeguard your wealth and ensure you're financially ready for life's major milestones.

Key Life Transitions to Plan For:

Marriage

- Marriage often brings financial decisions that need to be made jointly, such as merging finances, deciding on budgeting strategies, and managing debt.
- Be open about financial goals and establish clear communication about money from the start.

Children

- Children bring new financial responsibilities, including healthcare costs, childcare, education savings, and the increased cost of living.
- Begin planning for these expenses early and adjust your budget and insurance coverage as necessary.

Retirement

- Planning for retirement is crucial to maintaining your wealth throughout your later years. Start contributing to retirement accounts early to benefit from compound interest.

- Consider how your retirement income will be structured and make adjustments to your investments to ensure a steady income in retirement.

How to Prepare for Life Transitions:

- **Financial Planning**: Update your financial plan each time you encounter a significant life event.
- **Insurance Adjustments**: Ensure your insurance coverage is updated to reflect new responsibilities (e.g., life insurance for children or spouse).
- **Estate Planning**: Start building your estate plan to address how your assets will be distributed upon your death.

Actionable Step: Anticipate your next life transition and make a list of the financial adjustments you need to prepare for.

Establishing a Will and Estate Plan

Having a will and estate plan is crucial for ensuring your wealth is protected and passed on to your loved ones according to your wishes. Without a will, your estate may go through lengthy probate proceedings, leading to unnecessary stress and expenses for your family.

Key Components of an Estate Plan:

Will

- A will specifies how your assets will be distributed upon your death. This is the most basic form of estate

planning and is crucial for ensuring your family is taken care of.
- ➤ Make sure your will is updated regularly and includes instructions for guardianship if you have minor children.

Trusts

- ➤ Trusts can help you manage your wealth during your lifetime and ensure that your assets are distributed in accordance with your wishes after death.
- ➤ Trusts can also help avoid probate and minimize estate taxes.

Power of Attorney and Health Care Proxy

- ➤ These legal documents ensure that someone you trust can make financial or medical decisions for you if you're unable to do so.

Beneficiary Designations

- ➤ Make sure all your retirement accounts, life insurance policies, and other assets with beneficiary designations are up to date.

Actionable Step: Schedule a meeting with an estate planning attorney to create or update your will and ensure your estate is properly planned.

Staying Vigilant Against Fraud and Identity Theft

Fraud and identity theft are growing concerns that can significantly impact your wealth. Being vigilant and taking proactive measures can protect your financial security.

How to Protect Yourself from Fraud and Identity Theft:

Monitor Your Credit

- Regularly check your credit reports for any unauthorized activity. Use services like AnnualCreditReport.com to get free reports annually.
- Consider using credit monitoring services to receive alerts about suspicious activity.

Be Cautious with Personal Information

- Avoid sharing personal information, especially online or with unsolicited callers.
- Use strong passwords and enable two-factor authentication for added security on your financial accounts.

Shred Sensitive Documents

- Shred documents that contain sensitive information, such as your Social Security number, bank account details, and credit card information.

Actionable Step: Take steps to monitor your credit and secure your financial information. Consider setting up credit alerts and regularly reviewing your accounts for any unusual activity.

Final Thoughts

Protecting your wealth is just as important as building it. By understanding the financial risks you face and taking proactive steps to mitigate them, you can ensure that your wealth remains secure in the face of life's uncertainties. Insurance, diversification, estate planning, and vigilant monitoring are all crucial elements of a robust wealth protection strategy. Stay proactive, and your financial future will be far more secure.

Part 4: Sustaining Your Wealth Habit

Chapter 10
Automating Your Finances for Success

In today's fast-paced world, managing your finances manually can be overwhelming. It's easy to forget a bill, miss a savings deposit, or let investments fall by the wayside. This is where automation comes in—streamlining your financial processes to ensure consistency, discipline, and ease. By automating certain aspects of your financial life, you can focus on the bigger picture while ensuring your money works for you automatically. In this chapter, we'll explore the benefits of financial automation and how you can set up systems that support your wealth-building journey with minimal manual effort.

Benefits of Financial Automation

Automation is not just about making life easier—it's a powerful tool that can enhance your financial success in several ways. By automating certain financial tasks, you create a system that works for you without having to rely on willpower or memory.

Key Benefits of Financial Automation:

Consistency

One of the most significant benefits of automation is the ability to ensure that important financial tasks, such as paying bills or contributing to savings, happen on time every time. You don't have to remember to make payments or transfers—you simply set them up once and let automation take care of the rest.

Eliminates Human Error

Manual processes leave room for mistakes, whether it's miscalculating the amount of a payment or forgetting a bill altogether. Automation eliminates this risk, ensuring that your payments and transfers are accurate and on time.

Saves Time

Automating tasks like paying bills and transferring money into savings frees up your time for other important financial decisions or personal activities. You won't spend hours every month managing payments.

Enhances Financial Discipline

By setting up automatic transfers and payments, you establish a routine that aligns with your financial goals. This discipline ensures you are consistently saving, investing, and paying down debt without needing to think about it every month.

Improves Credit Score

Automating bill payments ensures that you never miss a due date, which helps you maintain a healthy credit score. On-time payments have a major impact on your credit score, and automation eliminates the risk of forgetting a payment.

Psychological Ease

Knowing that your finances are handled automatically brings peace of mind. You don't have to worry about managing multiple bills, and you can enjoy the confidence that your wealth-building habits are being maintained seamlessly.

Actionable Step: Identify one area of your finances that you can automate today. This might be a bill payment, savings transfer, or even a recurring investment. Set it up to get started with automating your finances.

Automating Bill Payments and Savings Contributions

A key component of financial automation is automating your regular expenses and savings. This ensures that your financial obligations are met without effort, while simultaneously building your savings.

Automating Bill Payments:

Set Up Automatic Bill Pay

1. Most service providers—whether for utilities, subscriptions, or credit card payments—allow you to set up automatic bill payments. By using this feature, you can ensure that your bills are always paid on time, avoiding late fees or missed payments.
2. Use your bank's online banking platform or third-party services like Mint or You Need a Budget (YNAB) to schedule recurring payments.

Choose the Right Payment Method

Use a credit card or a bank account for automatic payments. For bills that fluctuate in amount (e.g., utilities), many services allow you to schedule a fixed monthly payment to avoid unexpected charges.

Track Payments and Confirm Transactions

Even though the payments are automated, make sure to monitor your accounts to ensure that everything is being processed correctly. Regularly check your payment history to verify the amounts and due dates.

Actionable Step: Choose one or two recurring bills that you currently pay manually and set up automatic payments for them. This could be for your internet, phone, or utility bills.

Automating Savings Contributions:

Create Recurring Transfers to Savings Accounts

- ➢ Set up an automatic transfer from your checking account to your savings account each time you get paid. This "pay yourself first" method ensures that you prioritize saving before spending.
- ➢ Start small and gradually increase the amount over time as your income grows.

Automate Retirement Contributions

If you're contributing to a 401(k), IRA, or other retirement accounts, set up automatic contributions. Many employers offer automatic 401(k) deductions, or you can establish an automatic transfer to an IRA or brokerage account.

By automating retirement savings, you reduce the temptation to spend the money elsewhere.

Emergency Fund Automation

Build your emergency fund by automating small, regular deposits. Start with a set amount each week or month and adjust as necessary until you reach your emergency fund target (typically three to six months of living expenses).

Consider using a high-yield savings account to maximize interest on your emergency savings.

Actionable Step: Set up an automatic transfer to a savings or retirement account. Commit to depositing a percentage of your income, no matter how small, to ensure consistency.

Setting Recurring Investment Schedules

Investing is another area where automation can work wonders. Rather than waiting for the "perfect moment" to invest, automating your investment contributions ensures that you're consistently growing your wealth.

The Power of Dollar-Cost Averaging:

What is Dollar-Cost Averaging?

Dollar-cost averaging is the practice of investing a fixed amount of money into an investment at regular intervals, regardless of the price. This approach reduces the impact of market volatility by buying more shares when prices are low and fewer shares when prices are high.

Automation makes this process effortless and allows you to avoid trying to time the market.

Setting Up Automatic Contributions to Investment Accounts

- If you're using investment platforms like Vanguard, Fidelity, or Schwab, you can set up automated contributions to your brokerage or retirement accounts.
- Decide on a fixed amount that aligns with your financial goals and schedule it to be invested monthly or bi-weekly. This ensures you're investing regularly without having to remember each time.

Choosing the Right Investment Products

- Consider low-cost, diversified investment products like index funds or ETFs. These options allow for broad market exposure, minimizing risk while maximizing growth potential.
- Use automated investment platforms like Betterment or Wealthfront if you want a hands-off approach with professional management.

Actionable Step: Set up an automatic investment schedule for your retirement account or brokerage account. Decide how much you will invest monthly, and choose a diversified investment option.

Leveraging Technology to Minimize Manual Effort

With technology continually advancing, there are numerous apps, tools, and systems designed to help you manage and automate your finances with ease. From budgeting apps to investment platforms, technology can streamline the entire financial management process.

Top Financial Automation Tools:

Budgeting Apps

Use apps like Mint, YNAB, or PocketGuard to automatically track your spending, categorize your expenses, and keep an eye on your budget. These apps can link to your bank accounts and credit cards, automatically pulling in transactions for analysis.

Savings Apps

Apps like Digit and Qapital automate savings by rounding up your purchases to the nearest dollar and transferring the change into your savings account. These apps make saving effortless and can help you build an emergency fund or achieve other financial goals.

Investment Platforms

Platforms like Betterment, Acorns, or Wealthfront allow you to automate your investments based on your risk tolerance and financial goals. They provide simple, low-cost options for growing your wealth with minimal effort.

Automatic Bill Pay Services

Beyond your bank's automatic payment feature, services like Prism or Truebill help you manage all your bills and subscriptions in one place. These tools remind you of due dates, track your payments, and even allow you to negotiate lower bills.

Actionable Step: Research and choose at least one financial automation tool that will simplify your financial processes. This could be an app for budgeting, saving, or investing.

Avoiding Over-Reliance on Automation by Periodic Reviews

While automation is incredibly useful, it's essential to avoid becoming entirely hands-off. Automation is a tool to enhance your financial discipline, but you still need to review your financial situation periodically to ensure everything is on track.

Why Periodic Reviews Are Necessary:

Changes in Income or Expenses

Your financial situation may change over time. A raise, a new expense, or an unexpected windfall may require you to adjust your automated transfers or investment contributions.

Periodically reviewing your accounts ensures your financial system is still aligned with your goals.

Assessing Your Financial Goals

Over time, your financial goals may shift. Perhaps you've paid off significant debt, or you're now focused on building a larger investment portfolio. Periodic reviews help ensure your automated systems align with your evolving financial priorities.

Avoiding Overdraft Fees or Shortfalls

Automation can sometimes lead to overlooked transactions, like automatic subscriptions that you no longer use or over-automating your savings to the point where you don't have enough cash for day-to-day expenses. Regular reviews ensure you don't encounter any surprises.

Actionable Step: Set a reminder to review your financial accounts every 3-6 months. Make sure your automatic systems are still aligned with your goals and that you're not over-relying on automation.

Examples of Systems That Sustain Financial Discipline

To help you visualize how automation can work for you, here are a few examples of systems that can sustain financial discipline and support your wealth-building journey:

System 1: The "Set It and Forget It" Strategy

- ➢ Automate bill payments, savings transfers, and investments to be made on the same day each month.

This takes the guesswork out of your finances and helps you stay consistent in building wealth.

System 2: The "Wealth-Building Machine"

Set up automatic contributions to a diversified portfolio and retirement accounts. Use a budgeting app to track and categorize your spending, ensuring that every dollar is working toward your financial goals.

System 3: The "Emergency Fund Builder"

Automate weekly contributions to your emergency fund and set up savings apps that round up purchases to save extra change. Before you know it, you'll have a robust safety net to rely on.

Actionable Step: Identify a financial system you can automate today, such as a recurring savings transfer or automated bill payment. Start small and build from there.

Final Thoughts

Automation is a powerful tool for ensuring that your finances are consistently managed and aligned with your wealth-building goals. By automating bill payments, savings, investments, and budgeting, you free up mental energy and reduce the risk of human error. However, periodic reviews are necessary to ensure that your automated systems remain effective and aligned with your evolving financial goals. With automation in place, you'll be able to maintain financial discipline effortlessly while steadily progressing toward your financial freedom.

Chapter 11
Tracking Progress and Adjusting Strategies

Achieving financial success isn't a one-time event—it's an ongoing journey that requires consistent evaluation, adjustment, and fine-tuning. Tracking your progress and making necessary changes ensures that you remain on course toward your goals and adapt to any new challenges or opportunities that arise. In this chapter, we'll dive into how you can establish a routine for financial check-ins, assess what's working (and what isn't), avoid common pitfalls like lifestyle inflation, and celebrate your wins along the way. Staying proactive with your finances will keep you motivated and moving toward lasting wealth.

Establishing a Routine for Financial Check-Ins

Just as you wouldn't leave your car's maintenance to chance, you shouldn't let your financial situation run unchecked. Regular financial check-ins are essential for staying on top of your progress, ensuring you're not veering off track, and making adjustments as needed.

Why Financial Check-Ins Matter:

Catch Issues Early

A regular review allows you to spot potential issues early—whether it's a rising debt balance, missed payments, or declining investments. The sooner you notice these, the sooner you can correct them.

Track Goal Progress

Financial check-ins help you measure how far you've come in achieving your goals. Whether you're working on saving for a down payment, paying off debt, or growing an investment portfolio, you can track your progress and adjust your tactics if necessary.

Build Financial Discipline

Setting aside time to check in on your finances helps you stay disciplined and focused. You'll become accustomed to actively managing your financial life, which reinforces the wealth-building habits you've developed.

How to Set Up Regular Check-Ins:

Schedule Monthly or Quarterly Reviews

- ❖ Make it a habit to review your finances at least once a month. If you prefer, quarterly reviews allow you to take a broader view and adjust your strategies. The key is consistency.

Use a Checklist for Each Review

- ❖ Have a financial check-in checklist to ensure you cover everything: income, expenses, debt progress, savings, investments, and credit score.

Make It a Routine

- ❖ Schedule your reviews at the same time each month or quarter—perhaps at the end of the month or after receiving your paycheck. Consistency is key for making these check-ins part of your financial routine.

Actionable Step: Set a calendar reminder to review your finances once a month. Use a checklist to track all aspects of your financial health, from income and expenses to investments and credit.

Analyzing What's Working and What's Not

Tracking your progress is only valuable if you use the information to adjust and improve. A major part of financial check-ins is analyzing what's working and what's not—so you can amplify your successes and adjust your strategies when necessary.

How to Analyze Your Financial Progress:

Review Your Financial Statements

- ❖ Start by reviewing your bank statements, credit card statements, and investment reports. Are you staying within budget? Is your debt decreasing? Are your investments growing?

Evaluate Each Goal

For each financial goal you set, ask yourself:

- ➢ Am I on track to achieve this goal by the target date?
- ➢ If not, what needs to change?
- ➢ What are the obstacles I've encountered, and how can I overcome them?

Assess Your Spending Habits

Are you sticking to your budget, or are there areas where overspending has occurred? Identifying the categories where you're spending more than planned can help you make adjustments.

Adjusting Your Strategy:

Fine-Tune Your Budget

If you find that you're spending too much in certain categories, tighten your budget and consider reallocating funds to prioritize your savings, debt repayment, or investments.

Increase Your Savings Rate

If your income has increased, consider saving more each month rather than expanding your lifestyle. Look at your savings goals and determine whether you can increase your contributions to meet them faster.

Evaluate Investment Performance

If your investments aren't performing as expected, consider whether your strategy needs to be adjusted. A reallocation or diversification might be in order, especially if market conditions have changed.

Actionable Step: During your next financial check-in, take a close look at your current strategies. Identify areas where you're succeeding and areas that need adjustment. Don't be afraid to pivot if something isn't working.

Reassessing Goals as Circumstances Change

Your financial life doesn't exist in a vacuum—it's constantly evolving based on changes in your personal circumstances, external factors (such as the economy), and shifts in your priorities. Reassessing your financial goals ensures that they remain relevant and achievable, even as life changes.

When to Reassess Your Goals:

Major Life Changes

Events like getting married, having children, changing jobs, or buying a house are significant life changes that may require a reevaluation of your financial goals. These milestones can drastically impact your budget, income, and long-term objectives.

Shifting Priorities

Over time, your goals may change. Perhaps paying off debt is no longer your main priority, and you're now focused on saving for retirement or building wealth through investments.

Economic Factors

Fluctuations in the economy, such as inflation, job market shifts, or changes in interest rates, may also influence your financial goals. For instance, you might need to adjust your savings targets or investment strategies to account for these changes.

How to Reassess Your Goals:

Be Flexible

Understand that your goals should be flexible. Life will throw curveballs, and you'll need to adapt your goals accordingly. If a major life event occurs, don't be afraid to adjust your timeline or the amount you're contributing toward a specific goal.

Revisit Your SMART Goals

If your circumstances have changed, revisit your SMART goals (Specific, Measurable, Achievable, Relevant, Time-bound) and determine if they still make sense. Adjust the timeline, amount, or even the goal itself as necessary.

Actionable Step: If any major life events or changes in your circumstances have occurred recently, take time to reassess your financial goals. Adjust your strategies and timelines accordingly to ensure they still align with your new reality.

Avoiding Lifestyle Inflation While Increasing Income

As your income grows, there's often a temptation to increase your spending to match it—this is known as lifestyle inflation. While it's normal to want nicer things when you earn more, it's important to resist the urge to inflate your lifestyle to the point where you're not building wealth.

What is Lifestyle Inflation?

Definition and Examples

❖ Lifestyle inflation happens when you spend more money as your income rises. For example, you may upgrade your car, rent a more expensive apartment, or splurge on luxury items because you're now earning more.

The Risks of Lifestyle Inflation

❖ If you let lifestyle inflation take over, you'll end up in the same financial position despite earning more money. This prevents you from saving or investing as much as you could, slowing your wealth-building progress.

How to Avoid Lifestyle Inflation:

Increase Savings, Not Spending

❖ As your income increases, put the extra money toward savings, investments, or paying down debt. Aim to increase your savings rate rather than increasing your standard of living.

Set Up "Income Splits"

❖ When you receive a raise, allocate a portion of it to savings and another portion to investments. You may allow a small portion to increase your spending, but the majority should go toward building wealth.

Actionable Step: If you've recently received a raise or bonus, don't automatically spend the extra income.

Instead, allocate a percentage toward savings, investments, and debt repayment.

Celebrating Successes to Stay Motivated

Financial progress can sometimes feel slow, but every milestone you reach is an accomplishment that deserves recognition. Celebrating your financial wins, big or small, can keep you motivated and reinforce positive financial habits.

Why Celebrating Success Matters:

Boosts Motivation

- ❖ Acknowledging your progress, whether you've paid off a credit card, reached a savings goal, or increased your income, boosts motivation. This positive reinforcement makes you feel good about your financial journey and keeps you on track.

Increases Accountability

- ❖ Celebrating achievements also increases your accountability. It's easier to stay committed when you take time to acknowledge the hard work you've put in.

Ways to Celebrate:

Treat Yourself (Within Reason)

- ❖ Celebrate a milestone by doing something enjoyable, like having a nice meal out or taking a weekend trip.

Just make sure it's within your budget and doesn't detract from your financial goals.

Share Your Achievements

- ❖ Share your progress with friends, family, or your accountability partner. Their positive feedback and encouragement will reinforce your commitment to your financial goals.

Actionable Step: Set aside time to celebrate your financial wins, whether it's hitting a savings milestone, paying off a debt, or reaching an investment target. Reward yourself in a way that aligns with your financial goals.

Seeking Feedback from Mentors or Accountability Partners

One of the best ways to stay on track with your financial goals is to surround yourself with people who can provide guidance, feedback, and support. Whether it's a mentor, financial advisor, or accountability partner, having someone to check in with can keep you motivated and provide valuable insights.

Finding an Accountability Partner:

Benefits of Accountability

- ❖ Having someone to discuss your financial progress with can help you stay focused and accountable. This person can help keep you on track, encourage you when you face challenges, and celebrate your successes.

How to Choose the Right Partner

❖ Look for someone who shares your financial values, goals, and mindset. Ideally, this person should have experience in personal finance and be committed to providing honest feedback and encouragement.

Actionable Step: Identify a mentor or accountability partner who can help keep you motivated and offer guidance as you work toward your financial goals.

Final Thoughts

Tracking your progress and adjusting your strategies is a critical part of building lasting wealth. By establishing regular financial check-ins, analyzing what's working (and what's not), reassessing your goals, avoiding lifestyle inflation, and celebrating successes, you can stay motivated and on track for long-term success. Keep adjusting, stay flexible, and continue seeking opportunities for growth, and you'll build the wealth you desire.

Chapter 12
Paying It Forward and Leaving a Legacy

As you progress along your financial journey, one of the most fulfilling aspects of building wealth is the ability to give back—whether it's through generosity, teaching others, or leaving a legacy. By passing on the knowledge, values, and financial practices that have helped you succeed, you not only enrich the lives of others but also ensure that the wealth you've built endures for generations. In this chapter, we'll explore the importance of generosity in sustaining wealth, how to teach financial literacy to those you care about, the impact of giving back to your community, and how to leave a lasting financial legacy.

The Role of Generosity in Sustaining Wealth

Generosity may seem counterintuitive when thinking about wealth building, but in reality, giving back can be one of the most powerful tools for sustaining and growing your financial success. The principle of abundance—the belief that there's always more to go around—shifts your perspective on money. Rather than hoarding it, you begin to see it as a tool to improve your own life and the lives of others.

Why Generosity Matters:

Attracting Abundance

- ❖ By giving freely, you open the doors for more wealth and opportunities to flow into your life. Generosity breeds gratitude and attracts positive energy, leading to more prosperity.

Building Meaning and Purpose

❖ Money alone can't provide a sense of fulfillment. Giving to others—whether it's through charity, gifts, or volunteerism—adds deeper meaning to your wealth, reinforcing its purpose.

Strengthening Relationships

❖ Generosity creates stronger bonds with the people around you. When you share your wealth, whether through material gifts or time, you deepen relationships and establish a network of trust and support.

How to Integrate Generosity into Your Life:

Donate Regularly

❖ Set aside a percentage of your income for charitable donations, whether to causes you care about or to organizations that promote financial literacy.

Volunteer Your Time and Expertise

❖ Offer your time and skills to causes that align with your values. Volunteering allows you to give without a financial exchange but still make a significant impact.

Support Others on Their Journey

❖ Help those close to you by offering financial guidance, mentorship, or even small acts of kindness like helping with an emergency expense.

Actionable Step: Allocate a portion of your monthly income to charitable giving or volunteer work. Whether it's a set percentage or an ongoing project, make generosity a consistent part of your life.

Teaching Financial Literacy to Others, Including Family

One of the most important ways to leave a lasting legacy is by passing on financial knowledge to the people who matter most. Teaching financial literacy—whether to your children, relatives, or friends—ensures that the wealth-building habits you've cultivated will continue to thrive long after you're gone.

Why Financial Literacy is a Powerful Gift:

Empowering Others

❖ By teaching others how to manage money effectively, you're empowering them to build their own wealth and achieve their financial goals. Financial literacy is one of the most valuable tools for independence.

Breaking Cycles of Financial Struggle

❖ Many families pass down financial struggles from generation to generation due to a lack of education. By sharing the knowledge you've gained, you can help others break free from these cycles.

Creating Financial Confidence

- ❖ When others understand how to manage money, they feel more confident about making financial decisions, which leads to healthier attitudes towards money and wealth building.

How to Teach Financial Literacy:

Start Early

- ❖ Introduce the basics of money management to your children at an early age. Teach them about saving, budgeting, and investing in simple, practical ways.

Create a Family Financial Plan

- ❖ Involve your family in the financial planning process. Hold family discussions about goals, budgeting, and savings so everyone can understand the importance of financial responsibility.

Lead by Example

- ❖ Practice what you preach. Be a role model by demonstrating sound financial habits—whether that's sticking to a budget, saving regularly, or investing for the future.

Actionable Step: Take time to teach financial literacy to your family members. Consider setting up a weekly "money talk" with your kids or planning a financial education session for relatives.

Giving Back to Your Community Through Donations or Volunteering

Building wealth isn't just about accumulating money — it's about making a positive impact in the world around you. Giving back to your community through donations or volunteer work not only enriches others but also reinforces your own sense of purpose and fulfillment.

The Power of Community Giving:

Building Stronger Communities

- ❖ When you contribute to your community, you help create a thriving environment where people are supported and uplifted. Whether it's through donations, time, or resources, giving back builds connections that benefit everyone.

Fostering Social Responsibility

- ❖ As you become more successful, you have a responsibility to use your resources to address social issues, whether that's through charity work, local community efforts, or global causes.

Making a Difference

- ❖ Your donations — whether small or large — can make a real difference in someone's life. Volunteering your time or providing financial support can help those in need and create opportunities for others to succeed.

How to Give Back:

Support Causes You're Passionate About

- ❖ Choose causes that resonate with your values and passions. Whether it's education, homelessness, or environmental sustainability, find ways to support causes that align with your mission.

Donate Resources, Not Just Money

- ❖ Giving doesn't always mean handing over cash. Consider donating your time, skills, or goods to organizations that need your help.

Encourage Others to Get Involved

- ❖ Use your position of influence to inspire others to give back. Whether it's by volunteering together or encouraging colleagues to donate, spread the message of community support.

Actionable Step: Identify a local charity or community initiative you're passionate about, and commit to donating time, money, or resources on a regular basis. Invite friends or family to join you in giving back.

Building Generational Wealth and Passing Down Financial Values

True wealth isn't just about what you have; it's about what you pass on. Building generational wealth ensures that your legacy of financial wisdom, discipline, and success continues to impact your descendants for years to come.

Why Generational Wealth Matters:

Financial Freedom for Future Generations

- ❖ By building generational wealth, you give your children, grandchildren, and even great-grandchildren a head start in life, allowing them to pursue their passions, start businesses, or invest in their own futures without the burden of financial struggle.

Preserving Family Values

- ❖ Passing down not just assets but also the values and lessons that led to financial success is crucial. Your children and grandchildren will carry those lessons forward into their own lives.

Breaking the Cycle of Poverty

- ❖ Generational wealth can break cycles of financial hardship, allowing future generations to thrive and make better financial decisions than their predecessors.

How to Build and Pass Down Generational Wealth:

Create a Trust or Estate Plan

- ❖ Work with an estate planner to create a trust or will that ensures your assets are passed down according to your wishes. This protects your wealth and provides a clear path for future generations.

Teach Wealth-Building Principles Early

- Introduce your children or grandchildren to the principles of wealth-building while they're young. Teach them about saving, investing, and making smart financial decisions from an early age.

Invest in Future Opportunities

- Consider investing in educational opportunities for your descendants, such as funding college savings accounts or teaching them about entrepreneurship.

Actionable Step: Start by setting up an estate plan or trust that outlines how you want your assets to be distributed. Include your children or heirs in financial discussions and educate them about your approach to money.

Writing a Personal Wealth Manifesto

A wealth manifesto is a personal declaration of your values, principles, and goals when it comes to money. Writing one can help you solidify your commitment to wealth-building and establish a framework for how you want to manage and distribute your wealth.

Why a Wealth Manifesto Matters:

Clarifies Your Values

- A wealth manifesto helps you define what wealth means to you and how you intend to use it. It brings clarity to your financial decisions and ensures they align with your long-term goals.

Serves as a Guiding Document

- ❖ It acts as a compass, helping you stay focused on your wealth-building mission. Whenever you face a tough decision, you can return to your manifesto to guide you.

Establishes a Legacy

- ❖ A wealth manifesto also serves as a written record of your financial philosophy for future generations, ensuring that they understand and follow your principles.

How to Write Your Wealth Manifesto:

Define Your Purpose

- ❖ What is the purpose of your wealth? Is it to provide for your family? To give back to your community? To leave a legacy? Clarify your "why."

List Your Financial Principles

- ❖ Write down the principles that guide your financial decisions—things like saving, investing, living below your means, and giving back.

Set Specific Goals

- ❖ Detail your financial goals in your manifesto—whether it's saving a certain amount, becoming debt-free, or building generational wealth.

Actionable Step: Sit down and write your own personal wealth manifesto. Use it as a guiding document for your financial decisions and revisit it regularly to ensure you're staying true to your mission.

Inspiring Others with Your Financial Journey

Your financial journey has the potential to inspire others. As you build wealth and pay it forward, you not only improve your own life but also set an example for those around you. By sharing your story—both the successes and the challenges—you can motivate others to take control of their finances and pursue their own wealth-building goals.

How Your Story Can Inspire Others:

Sharing Your Struggles and Triumphs

- ❖ People connect with real, authentic stories. By sharing the ups and downs of your financial journey, you make it easier for others to believe they can succeed too.

Encouraging Financial Independence

- ❖ Your example of financial discipline and growth can inspire others to take charge of their finances and start their own journey toward financial freedom.

Creating a Ripple Effect

❖ As you inspire others to improve their financial situation, they, in turn, will inspire others. The impact of your story can create a ripple effect that spreads across communities and generations.

Actionable Step: Share your financial journey with others—whether it's through social media, blog posts, or personal conversations. Inspire someone else to take the first step toward financial freedom.

Final Thoughts

Paying it forward and leaving a legacy are the ultimate expressions of financial success. By being generous, teaching others, giving back to your community, and building generational wealth, you ensure that your wealth-building journey impacts not only your own life but also the lives of many others. Your financial legacy is a reflection of your values, and it has the power to shape future generations, making the world a better, more prosperous place for all.

Conclusion

The Wealth Habit for Life

As you reach the final pages of *The Wealth Habit*, you've come a long way. You've embarked on a powerful 6-week blueprint designed to transform your finances and set the foundation for lasting wealth. But while the journey outlined in this book may come to an end, your path toward financial freedom is just beginning.

Recap of the 6-Week Blueprint

Over the course of six weeks, we've focused on actionable steps to help you lay a solid financial foundation, take control of your finances, and build and protect wealth. Each chapter provided you with essential tools, practical advice, and strategies you can implement right away to start making real changes in your financial life. Here's a quick recap of what we've covered:

- **Week 1:** Defining your wealth vision and setting clear, actionable financial goals.
- **Week 2:** Assessing your current financial reality, identifying areas for improvement, and committing to your financial transformation.
- **Week 3:** Mastering the wealth mindset, breaking free from limiting beliefs, and cultivating a mindset for abundance and success.
- **Week 4:** Taking control of your finances through budgeting, debt reduction, and building a financial safety net.
- **Week 5:** Growing and protecting your wealth with smart investments, income diversification, and risk management strategies.

➢ **Week 6:** Automating your finances, tracking progress, and sustaining your wealth habit for long-term financial success.

By following this blueprint, you've established habits that will guide you toward lasting financial freedom. The most important part of this process is not just the actions you've taken during these six weeks, but the habits you've developed that will continue to grow and compound over time.

Encouragement to Embrace the Ongoing Journey

The 6-week plan was designed to get you started on the right track, but building lasting wealth is a lifelong journey. There will be new challenges to face, unexpected opportunities to seize, and adjustments to make as your circumstances evolve. The key is to remain flexible, keep learning, and continually reinforce the habits that have brought you this far.

Financial freedom doesn't happen overnight. It's built on consistent, small actions that add up over time. The habits you've learned through this book—budgeting, investing, managing debt, and protecting your wealth—are tools that will serve you well for the rest of your life.

The Impact of Consistent Small Actions Over Time

One of the most important lessons from *The Wealth Habit* is that financial success is not about one big, life-changing event. It's about the small, daily actions that you take to improve your financial situation. Each time you save a little bit more, invest wisely, pay down debt, or avoid impulsive spending, you're making progress.

- **Small actions compound** over time: Just as small investments grow exponentially thanks to compound interest, your financial habits will pay off in ways that are often invisible in the short term, but incredibly powerful in the long run.
- **Consistency is key**: The people who succeed financially are the ones who commit to doing the right things day in and day out, even when it doesn't seem like much. The more you stick with it, the more it becomes second nature—and that's where true financial freedom begins.
- **Patience pays off**: Building wealth isn't about making drastic changes overnight. It's about staying the course, adjusting when necessary, and making steady progress toward your goals. Be patient with yourself, and trust the process.

Final Thoughts on Building a Life of Financial Freedom and Purpose

True financial freedom is about more than just money; it's about living with purpose. The wealth you build is meant to serve a larger purpose—whether it's to provide for your family, give back to your community, or live a life that aligns with your values. By integrating your financial journey with your greater purpose, you'll find that the pursuit of wealth becomes a means to an even greater end.

Your financial goals are not isolated; they are part of the bigger picture of who you are and the life you want to create. Whether it's securing a comfortable retirement, starting your own business, or creating a legacy for your children, financial freedom provides you with the tools to live life on your own terms.

Call to Action: Take the First Step Today

Now that you've learned the essentials for transforming your finances, it's time to take action. Start by reflecting on what you've learned and choose one area where you can make an immediate impact. Whether it's setting up a budget, reducing debt, or opening a retirement account, every step you take moves you closer to your goal.

Remember, this journey is about building the wealth habit for life. The first step might feel small, but as you continue to take action, the results will snowball.

Take the first step today. Commit to implementing just one of the strategies you've learned and make it part of your daily life. Whether it's tracking your expenses or setting up an automatic savings plan, start now. And remember, this is not a one-time thing—it's a lifelong habit that will serve you, your family, and future generations.

The journey toward financial freedom isn't a race. It's a path that's paved with consistent actions, perseverance, and a mindset that's rooted in abundance. By embracing *The Wealth Habit*, you've already set yourself on the right course. Keep moving forward, stay disciplined, and let your financial freedom unfold—one habit at a time.

Here's to your wealth, your future, and the lasting legacy you'll create.

Thank you for joining me on this transformative journey. Now, go ahead — take that first step and begin building the wealth habit that will change your life!

www.ingramcontent.com/pod-product-compliance
Lightning Source LLC
Chambersburg PA
CBHW050306230526
45471CB00005B/2042